The Rent-Free Solution

How to Stop Renting and Buy a Home in Des Moines and Live Rent Free!

By Tyler Osby

Copyright © 2014 Tyler Osby
All rights reserved.
ISBN-10: 1502855003
ISBN-13: 978-1502855008

Here's What's Inside...

- 5   Introduction
- 7   The Rent-Free Solution!
- 8   Why Don't More People Buy Homes?
- 9   The True Cost Difference between Renting and Owning a Home...
- 12 Here's How to Buy a Home and Live Rent-Free...
- 20 Why Don't More People Live Rent-Free...
- 22 Here Are Examples of People Who Have Done the Rent-Free Solution...
- 35 Why It's More Expensive to Rent than to Own a Home...
- 38 What to Do If You Have Credit Issues...
- 41 How Much Down Payment Do I Need?
- 43 How to Safeguard Yourself from Major Repairs...
- 52 How Much House Can I Afford?
- 54 The Difference between Being Pre-Qualified and Pre-Approved for a Home...
- 56 What Goes into a Mortgage Payment?

58 **Here's How the Rent-Free Solution Works...**

62 **Here's Exactly How to Stop Renting and Buy A Home in Des Moines and Live Rent Free...**

63 **About the Author**

Introduction

The Rent-Free Solution!
Des Moines, Iowa

A few years ago I had a huge *ah-ha* moment after reading the book *Rich Dad, Poor Dad*. The concepts covered in that book got me thinking about an entirely different way to own your first home, one that makes it significantly more attractive and with much less risk and liability. A way that truly makes your home an investment, not a liability (as the book described most people's homes they live in).

That's what this book is all about.

Over the past decade in the mortgage business, I've found that many people who are currently renting could be saving a lot of money by buying a home to live in. Yet, many people believe living in a home is more expensive than renting, or they think they can't afford a house, or they have concerns about not having a big enough down payment. The truth is all of these concerns may be common, but they're unwarranted.

You do not have to continue to pay rent every month to help pay off someone else's mortgage. You can be the one receiving money from other people to pay down your mortgage.

What follows is the transcript of a conversation between myself and a REALTOR where I talked about how you can avoid paying rent using *The Rent-Free*

Solution.

The Rent-Free Solution is a combination of ideas that came together to form a comprehensive strategy for living rent free.

I hope this book educates you and helps change your way of thinking about buying a home and encourages you to start living rent-free!

To Your Success!

Tyler Osby

The Rent-Free Solution!

Susan: Good morning this is Susan Austin. I'm super excited to be here today with Tyler Osby. Tyler is going to share with us how you can stop renting and buy a home in Des Moines and live rent free. Welcome Tyler.

Tyler: Thank you for having me, Susan. I'm excited as well.

Susan: Let's start with why did you want to write this book?

Tyler: There are a lot of people that could become home owners but they have certain reservations. They don't believe you can actually own a home and not have to pay the mortgage. It is a unique strategy that I came across several years ago and have had many clients take advantage of it. It has been really fun to see those people make the transition from renting to owning their own home and not be burdened with a large mortgage payment. I feel like this is a message that needed to get out there because there really isn't anyone else pulling back the curtain so to speak on this concept and really unpack how to do it. I figured this will be a good way to facilitate that process for people, and I want to get the word out and share it with people, so more people can be successful home owners.

Susan: I've never heard of anyone talk about how you can own a home and live rent free. That's pretty exciting.

Tyler: I think a lot of people feel the same way.

Why Don't More People Buy Homes?

Susan: What are some of the reasons people aren't buying homes?

Tyler: We hear a lot of the reasons why they don't want to buy a home. Some people think you need a large down payment to be able to buy a home, and therefore they think they can't afford to buy one.

They think you need as much as 20% down which as we'll show just isn't the case. Other people think renting is just cheaper than owning a home, so they think they are saving money every month when that isn't the case either.

Some people think owning a home is risky, and they like the safety and security of renting, when really very much the opposite is true. A lot of people think in order to buy a home they have to plan on living in that home for a really long time to recoup the expense, so if they are unsure about how long they will be in one place they opt to not buy a home. There are some surprising details on why that is not always true.

Then some people think they need to be married or have kids or be further along in life to be home owners. Finally, some people think it takes pristine credit to qualify to purchase a home which is not always true. We hear a lot of different reasons about why people don't want to become home owners, and hopefully I'll shed some light on why most of the reasons don't always hold water any longer.

The True Cost Difference between Renting and Owning a Home...

Susan: What are some of the advantages of home ownership, Tyler?

Tyler: If you're renting a home or apartment what you're doing is each month you write a check to your landlord; you're actually paying your landlord's mortgage, taxes, insurance and repairs for him/her. I know this from personal experience because I've done some very, very large loans for major landlords here in Des Moines area. When you're a renter you're helping pay someone else's mortgage, and that's the first thing I want renters to understand. When you rent, you are actually paying someone else's mortgage for them. So in effect even though you are only renting, you are simply making the mortgage payment that someone else owns and gets the benefit from.

Let me share an example to illustrate this point. If you rent for five years at $800 a month, you'll spend $48,000 in rent payments over that period.

Susan: Wow! That's more than I would have thought.

Tyler: I know, right? Whereas if you were a home owner you would be able to own the home that you live in, you would pay the same money on a monthly basis, and likely less if you follow through the suggestion we're going to talk about in here in *The Rent-Free Solution*.

During those five years if you owned your own home, you would have the benefits of the home value increasing, while also gaining the benefits of paying down the balance on the mortgage over those five years. So your equity goes up higher and higher as you also pay down the mortgage every month.

There are also some very cool tax advantages of owning a home where you can get a larger tax refund each year due to getting a mortgage interest deduction. Home ownership offers a lot of really cool things to people, and I want more people to be able to experience this. There's a reason rich people always buy their homes. Over time it's proven to be a great way to get ahead in the world with the added bonus of saving money on your taxes.

Honestly when you rent, in most cases you're living in a noisy apartment building where you have noisy neighbors coming home at 2am. You have a landlord who doesn't want to fix things that break. There are just so many different things you have to deal with when you rent.

Whereas if you own your home, you have pride of home ownership; it's your place; you can paint the walls the way you want them; you can live the way you want and you don't have to worry about noisy neighbors coming in and out at 2am either.

Susan: Plus there's something to not having to move every few years when you own a home.

Tyler: Even if you do move, you're not getting robbed of all that rent money every month. Think of it as paying yourself instead of paying the landlord. As a home owner you get so many advantages of owning a home.

Here's How to Buy a Home and Live Rent-Free...

Susan: Can you share with us how *The Rent-Free Solution* works?

Tyler: Housing expense tends to be the largest expense people have. Student loans are starting to catch up with that number, depending on the situation, but for the most part paying for where you live every month is your largest expense. *The Rent-Free Solution* is a combination of ideas I've run across which came together to really form a great strategy.

There is a book I read a really long time ago called *Rich Dad, Poor Dad*. You probably have heard of it. It's by Robert Kiyosaki. If you enjoy the topic of money and real estate you might be inspired by this book like I was.

The book talks about how most people treat their home as an asset meaning it is a benefit on their balance sheet so to speak. The disappointing truth to this however, is most people work the first two weeks of the month to pay for their house payment. That's a shockingly high number. People are working a lot to just pay for their house. What would it look like if that wasn't the case? I started doing some thinking, and what I came up with was the concept of having other people pay your mortgage for you.

In the *Rich Dad, Poor Dad* book they talk about using "other people's money" which is OPM. Say you bought a home that is a duplex. A duplex is a home where there are two sides to it. Each side of the duplex has three bedrooms. A three bedroom home would rent out on its own for between $800 to $1000 a month here in Des Moines, Iowa. And let's say for owning that duplex you have a house payment of $1,400. You put a renter into half of the duplex, and you have a renter who pays you $900 a month. That effectively brings your mortgage payment down to $500; which is actually fantastic in itself.

Imagine being able to live in your own home for $500 a month? That is less, often by half, what people are already paying for rent. So not only do you get all the advantages of owning a home, you get to do it for less than what you are paying now in rent!

Susan: Oh, that's great Tyler.

Tyler: Yes, and this is where it gets exciting. We then we got to thinking what if we really made a big game change to this concept and we added a renter on your side of the duplex as well?

If you took one of the bedrooms in your half of the duplex and rented it out for say $400 a month, now what is your mortgage payment? Essentially $100 a month! That really changes things, doesn't it?

One of the beautiful things of The *Rent-Free Solution* is you're able to forgo that monthly rent expense, and it allows you to do other things with that money. For example, you could take the difference and aggressively pay down the mortgage on the home. You could easily have that home paid for in a fraction of the time just by paying what you are already paying for in rent!

Think about what a huge difference this would make in your life to have a paid for home you get to live in and other people are now writing you checks every month?

And even if you weren't interested in aggressively paying down the mortgage, you can do a lot of other things with the money you save from *The Rent-Free Solution*.

Maybe you have some debts you'd like to pay off. This could help you really speed up the process of becoming debt free. If you're already debt free, it could really speed up the process of being able to do a lot more with investing and creating more money for retirement or whatever your saving goals are. The sky's the limit.

Some of the people that we talk about in this book had actually used that extra cash flow to really have some unique experiences. One of them took a killer vacation that he would never have been able to afford otherwise. All from basically bringing their housing expense down to nothing or next to nothing.

The Rent-Free Solution is a fast track way to become a millionaire, and that's no exaggeration. If you talk to some of the smartest investment minds out there, they will say yes, owning a home is a huge part of becoming financially independent. What we are talking about here is being able to own a home which also becomes an investment - all the while getting to live in rent free. By doing this you would exponentially increase your results towards financial independence.

If you do a normal 30 year mortgage and get to live in the home rent free like we're talking about in this book, it really is like injecting the concept with some steroids. Say you pay the same amount you were paying while renting towards the mortgage payment. You'll own your home outright very quickly. Or you could sock away that extra money and build up a great savings. The Rent-Free Solution gives you so many different options that you wouldn't have otherwise. If you are in your 20's or 30's and have a paid off home, your life is going to change dramatically. Period, end of story.

It's going to be a big, big game changer for you if you decided to take this idea and run with it.

Susan: Not having to write that rent check every month, whether it's $800 or $1200, that's a pretty significant influx of cash for someone. You've got me excited! I want to hear more about this.

Tyler: Yes, I'm super excited about the concept, too. I've seen the real difference it can make in someone's life. Let's talk about how we can super-charge this strategy and look at what happens to the number when we add in a roommate to your side of the duplex.

Many people who have a roommate and a lot of them don't mind. It could be a significant other or a longtime friend. What if you were to rent a room at your three bedroom home that you now own to that friend? You can get $400 rent easy out of that person which now effectively brings your monthly payment down to $100 a month, which is insane!

What if we make this a little bit crazier and see what happens when we have two roommates on your side of the duplex, what would that look like? In that situation you could actually be earning $300 a month. So not only do you get to live rent free, you make money every month!

There are a lot of people who have this living arrangement while their renting and they don't mind it. They gladly write the check each month to live with two of their good friends and in this situation where you can be the person who owns the property, so you get to benefit from the arrangement and not some random landlord you and your friends never even meet.

Those two friends gladly pay you because they're sick of living in an apartment anyway, and they're able to help you pay the mortgage, but also you're getting a cash flow of $300 a month. This is where this idea becomes extremely exciting because not only are you living cheap, but you could even make money in this situation. That's The Rent-Free Solution and a couple of different ways of how you can approach it.

Susan: I love it because it doesn't necessarily have to be for a lifetime, you know?

Tyler: Not at all.

Susan: If you have high student loan debt or a big car payment or credit card debt, you can do this for five years, and I can imagine as you said, this concept becomes the rocket fuel of getting those debts paid off. Love it!

Tyler: This really eases someone into home ownership in a really creative and interesting way. The people who are really aggressive and want to have zero rent on a monthly basis don't have to pay anything. They can do that with the multiple roommate solution, and then as they become more and more independent, maybe they lose a roommate.

As your financial situations really change, you can evolve the plan. Eventually you just occupy one side and then have a tenant on the other side. The house payment is still only a few hundred dollars a month, and then eventually you could own the home as an investment property and rent out both sides. By renting out both sides, you have positive cash flow because you have $800 on each side coming in. Then you become an owner of rental property, and you can buy your next home.

Whether that is that next $300,000 home once you've become engaged or married, or maybe you've outgrown the duplex, and you need a larger home. As your life changes, you can change how you use the duplex to your advantage. This is a really cool way to become owner of investment property without the huge risk that a lot of investors take and also without the huge down payments that most investment property loans would require, which is another reason why this strategy is so sexy to me.

Susan: It used to be that you would start off with a really small starter home and then buy up from there. With The Rent-Free model, you've superseded that and shown us there's a way to get into the game faster with a bigger home. Your side of the duplex can be bigger than they can afford on their own.

Tyler: Yes and most cases these homes that you buy are much nicer than the old starter home type scenario that a lot of our parents grew up doing. We've really broken the model of a first time home buyer and made it a more obtainable outcome for more people.

Also the thing that excites me more than anything is this strategy playing out long term. This is really something that can make a huge impact on your retirement. Thirty years from now where are you going to be? You probably are going to be in retirement. What's that going to look like? If you own an investment property and you've got somebody who's paying you two grand a month and you own the home outright, that's a pretty cool retirement strategy.

It's not just you owning a home, which is exciting in itself. That's a major milestone for us Americans. We work hard to be able to own a home, but it's also a fast track to becoming a millionaire. The numbers support this.

This is also a cool retirement plan other people are funding for you. The home will appreciate in value over those 30 years, and you can then sell the home and have the cash or keep the monthly rent coming in.

Susan: There's so much meat on this bone, Tyler! You've come up with a solution which solves so many problems at once.

First of all, the American dream of owning a home has become a lot harder for a lot more people nowadays. We're not making as much it seems; everything seems to be a little bit more expensive. *The Rent-Free Solution* is a way to get into the game and really get ahead at the same time.

Here's a way to not only own the home, you've taken it further and by making it an investment and a place you can call home, and your kids can play in the back yard. That's really great. Two birds with one stone if you will. And you get to pick who lives next door!

Tyler: Exactly, and that's the key.

Susan: You can eventually have your aging parents living there. There's so many way this could play out.

Tyler: A lot of times people who live in rental situations generally have a neighbor they like, but they have a lot of neighbors that they dislike. You can pack up and leave your current rental with the neighbor you like and move them into your new duplex! It's really a win for everyone, and the perception from those friends' perspective is they see this person is willing to take the risk of owning a home and go with him. You as the person who's buying the home thinks, "I'm willing to take the risk because for this I'm actually lowering my expenses, I might even get paid in the deal." This is a really good long term investment for me as a home owner, so really that's all about everybody in the situation. I think that's what makes it so exciting.

Why Don't More People Live Rent-Free...

Susan: What do you think would stop someone from doing something like this?

Tyler: The number one reason is people don't realize it's possible. What you don't know, you don't know. I'm hopeful this book will not only show that the idea is out there, but specifically how to do it. As soon as you understand how this works, there will be a lot of people who never thought owning a home was possible. They will now become interested and hopefully start going down that path of what it could look like if we put this together.

Susan: What if there are no duplexes where you live?

Tyler: *The Rent-Free Solution* isn't something that only applies to duplexes. It works with single family homes as well, which is a standard stand alone house. This solution applies to any type of property. The duplex takes the idea and puts it on steroids. The base idea, if you want to call it that, is getting that starter home that our parents and grandparents talk about getting and having roommates in that starter home; that's kind of a step one.

If you want to put that idea on steroids, you would want to look at buying a duplex which is a situation where you have a home attached to another home. It is separated, but if you do that the duplex is going to be slightly more expensive, but your potential rental income is going to drastically increase making it possible to make your monthly payment less and even potentially have positive cash flow.

Meaning earning money on a monthly basis by having renters living next door to you and also roommates living with you, so there's a lot of different ways to execute this. It's not just one specific type of property. Some people may want to live in a certain area, and maybe there aren't duplexes in that area. Maybe they don't want to take care of the lawns; maybe a condo fits this more or a townhouse. The type of property isn't as important. It's just important that the potential rental income will help offset the mortgage payment.

Here Are Examples of People Who Have Done the Rent-Free Solution...

Susan: I love it. Let's talk about some examples: people you know that have gone through *The Rent-Free Solution*.

Tyler: For privacy of the clients I'll only use their first names.

The first person who comes to mind is a client who did this quite a while back when she bought a duplex. Her name was Courtney. Courtney bought the duplex in the western part of Des Moines, and it was three bedrooms on each side. The purchase price of the duplex was $191,000, and she put a real small down payment of three and half percent, which in her case happened to be gifted from a family member. The taxes on that property were $3,926 a year. Homeowners insurance covers against fire, theft, tornados, that kind of stuff, and was $873.96 a year. The total mortgage payment on her FHA loan was $1,529 a month, and the rent from the vacant non-Courtney occupied side of the home was $985.

Courtney then got a roommate who lived in one of the three bedrooms on her side and that roommate paid her $400 a month so her effective mortgage payment on that home was $144 a month so she went from paying I think almost a $1,000 a month in rent where she was living in Des Moines to bringing her payment down to $144 a month. She could even have an additional renter on her side where she's now making money on a monthly basis.

Courtney is a great success story. Because of buying this duplex and renting it out the way she has, she's really enjoyed the benefits of becoming a homeowner with *The Rent-Free Solution*.

Susan: Love it. And what's going to happen long term for Courtney?

Tyler: It's dramatic. The beauty of Des Moines is we're a very steady community, so you don't see huge appreciation in value, but at the same time you don't see a huge depreciation in home values. You just see things kind of steadily increase, so I can tell you right now that if you buy a home in Des Moines over time you will see a dramatic increase in value.

For Courtney's example, she bought the duplex for $191,000. If you go back seven years from when she bought it, it was bought for $174,000, and then if you go back 20 years it was bought for $64,000. In this particular case 20 years ago this duplex was $63,000. Now it's worth $191,000 that's a dramatic increase in equity for the home owner.

Susan: That's more than double. If Courtney hadn't bought a duplex but rather bought a single family residence that she lived in by herself, is there a difference in how much home she would have qualified for?

Tyler: That's a great question. To answer that question the best way to address it is if you own a home you're buying just to live in yourself, you will probably qualify for a lot less than you would if you had a renter in the other side of a duplex.

For example, let's say Courtney wasn't able to qualify for $191,000 on her own. It might be something more like a $150,000 on her own. So, if you're buying it as a potential to rent part of it, in a lot of cases you will be able to buy more home because of that. There might be people reading this that say well, I think I only qualify for a certain amount, but if you're employing *The Rent-Free Solution* you could potentially qualify for more house because part of that house is going to be paid for by someone else.

A lot of people are surprised once they start looking how inexpensive duplexes really are and how nice they are. It's very misleading. It's the predisposition people have about duplexes, but once you start seeing what's available, you see this isn't about sacrificing quality of lifestyle; it's about enhancing it.

The cool thing about Courtney's situation is when Courtney came to us, she told us there's a good chance that she'll be relocated from her job, and she has some reservations about buying a home. So we talked through it, and the reason why *The Rent-Free Solution*, which at the time didn't have a name by the way, came to mind was because I knew that if she were able to buy a duplex, and she relocated, she could easily hire a property management company who would find tenants and manage the tenants and manage the property. She could relocate to somewhere else and not only would that cover her mortgage payment, but she'd also still be making money as a property owner.

She could still be in Florida and still own property here in Des Moines, Iowa but it will all be taken care of and managed by someone else.

Susan: That alleviates some of the stress of someone who isn't sure how long they may be staying in Des Moines.

Tyler: I think it does.

Susan: That's why you said you should look at this home as both a home to live in and as an investment property. So if and when your life situation changes, you can simply move out of your half of the duplex, put someone else in there, and make even more money. Can you share with us another example?

Tyler: The second example is a client named Eric. Eric recently bought a duplex which has two bedrooms on each side, so it is a four bedroom home all together. The purchase price on that home was $162,000. The down payment on that home again was three and a half percent with an FHA loan. That down payment was also a gift from a family member. The amount of down payment was $5,670 and the taxes on that property were $3,956 and the annual home owners insurance was $1,067, so the total mortgage payment on this home for Eric was $1,376.

Now one side of the duplex rented out for $875 a month, and in Eric's situation, he actually bought the home with the tenant already leased out on the other side. He just took over that lease, and that has been great for him ever since, but they had already arranged to pay $875 a month; duplexes often have one side already rented.

Then he has a spouse who lives with him, and she has been contributing $400 a month into their joint account renting, so she was going to continue doing that once she moved into the duplex. His effective payment on that home when you consider all things in was just over a $100 a month.

I had talked with Eric about potentially renting out the other room in his duplex. At the time of closing he hadn't done it yet. If he did, he could easily collect another $400 from that making him an extra $300 each and every month. So not only does he not have to pay rent, he is actually pocketing money each month.

He's a business owner, so he wanted to find a home to live in that would allow him to have a little bit less impact on his monthly cash flow and grow his business. So this solution is allowing him the freedom to grow his business with less financial stress. It was really a fun opportunity to get him and his wife into a house and have an extremely low mortgage payment.

Susan: Well that's super exciting.

Tyler: When I first met with Eric he wanted to keep his mortgage payment to around $500 a month. I told him, "You know Eric, if you only want to pay $500 a month on your mortgage, you're going to end up with a crappy house on the wrong side of town." He would be looking at a house for around $50,000 if he wanted a payment around $500 a month.

He said, "I don't want to live in a $50,000 house; that's not going to be what we're looking for."

I said, "Well let me throw another idea at you." He was engaged to be married as we were talking, so he and his fiancée were interested in buying together. I said, "If you buy a duplex, and you rent out one side of the duplex, I think we can get your mortgage payment down to $500 a month." He said, "From my contribution, or for our contribution?" Then I said, "That's like your contribution together, so if your fiancée still wants to contribute a certain amount of money each month that is fantastic."

In his situation that's what ended up happening, so we were able to help him own a home that was significantly nicer than a $50,000 shack that they were forced to look at before *The Rent Free Solution* came into the picture.

Now he and his wife are effectively responsible for $500 a month, which is really incredible when you consider he was looking to own a home that was $50,000 versus a home that was $162,000.

Susan: That's a complete game changer.

Tyler: Even if you're not after a true rent-free type solution but you just want to have a really, really cheap house payment, we can achieve that using the same strategy. It's just a matter of how far you want to take your rent free solution because there are so many different levels of intensity.

Eric's duplex was located in Urbandale which is a nice suburb of Des Moines. So many people have made just a huge change in their life by following *The Rent-Free Solution*. I'm excited to be sharing it.

Susan: What if someone is not interested in a duplex?

Tyler: Right. A lot of people might be reading this and thinking I don't really want to buy a duplex. I'm not interested in owning a duplex. I want to have a single family home. They're not alone. There are a lot of people who would prefer to own a single family home over a duplex, and that's fine. *The Rent-Free Solution* will work for those people too. The way it works is not a whole different than it works on a duplex.

With a single family home, you just get roommates. A lot of people will pay $400 or more per month to live in a house and have a room and joint access to a bathroom, driveway or street parking. I've had clients who bought houses anywhere from $90,000 all the way up to $350,000 who rent out rooms to friends, and they have effectively made their mortgage payment very minimal in the name of a couple hundred dollars to one client actually making money renting out all these rooms to friends.

For those people, that's their dream come true experience. They want to have people live with them; they don't want to be just private, not have their friends around; these people really want to have people around. Single family homes are great way to achieve that.

Susan: Very good, and as you pointed out earlier, as your financial situation changes, you have the option of changing the arrangement. But now the mortgage is 50% paid off, or you have a bucket of money that you've saved by having roommates.

Tyler: Well that's the cool thing. Whether you buy a duplex or single family home or condo or a townhouse; all these types of homes can qualify as rent-free homes.

Ultimately, it is something where you can start out with this rent-free solution and do it for a short period of time to kind of ease into home ownership or meet your savings goals or pay off debt. Whatever your goal is then eventually if you want to be alone in this place and not have any other renters and just have a regular old mortgage payment like most people do, that's perfectly fine.

You're not committing to anything long term with the way that you do this. But it is a really nice way to transition from being a person who rents a home at a pretty high monthly expense, and a lot of cases as renter at record highs right now in Des Moines, to become a home owner while rates are at their all-time low and really save a lot of money.

Susan: What does the long game look like with this?

Tyler: A lot of us make these decisions with buying a home based on a short term need. You're sick of hearing the noisy neighbors, or you're just ready to move out of an apartment living situation. This is fantastic. That's a great reason to buy a house, but the really exciting part for me as a guy who's been doing this for 11 years now is seeing a long term impact of making these types of decisions. If you buy a home today, and you buy it using *The Rent-Free Solution* strategy, long term you could essentially have a retirement in the making.

If you live in a house, let's say you buy a house today with *The Rent-Free Solution*, and you live in it for 5 to 10 years, and then your living situation changes. Let's say you need some more space because you've got a couple of kids. You need more area for all that stuff and you've decided you need to buy a new house to do that. Now your property that was your primary property, that place that you've lived in becomes an investment property. Let's say it was a duplex, and you already have one half of that rented out. Well now that you're moving out of the one half, the other half becomes also something that you can rent out to someone else. You can rent that other side out, or if you live in a single family home you can rent out the other rooms, or just rent it out to one family, and you're on to buy your own next place. This property that you've lived in to begin with, your first home, is now an investment property where other people are paying your mortgage for you.

Depending on how aggressively you pay down that mortgage you can be mortgage free in as long as 30 years and as short as 10 years. As soon as that payment pays off the mortgage balance, that rent money continues to come in with major benefits having cash flow and other property ownership benefits like the property increasing in value.

I was talking a little while ago about Courtney with the place that sold like 20 years ago for $60,000 and now it's worth $191,000. Imagine where that's going in 20 and 30 years. That property value is going to be insane, so you could either live off the cash flow, which is what your monthly rent is versus what your expense will be. At that point the only thing you'll be paying is tax and insurance because you're not going to have a mortgage on it, or you can sell it as a piece of real estate that you own outright, and whatever you sell it for you can take the proceeds and do whatever you like with it.

It depends on how you want to play it, but a lot of people accumulate rental properties for the purposes of living off the cash flow that comes in off the rents each month. Other people buy rental properties to buy and hold, then sell eventually once the values are much higher. That's also something you can do.

Susan: This isn't an overnight get rich-quick scheme. Over time you get the benefit of using other people's money to pay down your mortgage. It may open you up to be open to even further investing. Are people only allowed to own one of these homes at a time?

Tyler: A lot of people think that's true that the lenders law may allow you to own one home at a time, but it's really just a self-limiting belief.

I have accumulated properties through the way of owning to occupy the home. Then each time I've gone to buy a new house, I've kept the old property as a rental property, so now I've got five homes in total. A lot of people have done the same thing.

You can also go about buying homes specifically as investment properties, but it's a different situation to do that. The benefits of owning a home to live in, first, is you'll get better interest rates and lower down payments. It's really just the cheapest way to accumulate property to live in.

There is absolutely no issue with having multiple properties. The cool thing is if you have a history of owning property you have a history of receiving income on that property through your tax returns. You're going to be able to offset your potential expense in qualifying for a loan by documenting that you've had income on the old properties.

Susan: Do they have to pay taxes on the rent that they collect every month?

Tyler: Well that's a really great question, and I want to lean on the help of a professional accountant or CPA for people to really reflect tax questions on. Rental income is taxable, but you start a new schedule on your tax return when you own rental property called the Schedule E.

On your Schedule E, you list off the total rents that you've had and then the total expenses that you've had. The total expenses including the mortgage payment, any utilities you're responsible for, taxes, homeowners insurance and really anything that falls into the expense category. Then there's this really fun tax thing called depreciation, which is basically saying this property is an investment, but it is also something that you acquired, so we're going to depreciate the value of the property over a certain amount of time.

Specifically for a duplex if you're occupying let's say half of it and the other half is investor property that's rented out to somebody, you would depreciate half of the value property over time, so the depreciation falls into the expense column. Usually after depreciation and other expenses there is no taxable income because the depreciation is such a large deduction on your tax return. I have to say that there are situations where you could have enough income where it becomes taxable, but it's still not a large consequence.

Susan: When you become mortgage free on this duplex, and let's say by that time rents are up, and they're paying you $1,500 a month; that is considered income, but that's $1,500 a month you wouldn't have otherwise so you can use some of that rent money to pay any taxes owed.

Tyler: Going back to the original source this concept of the *Rich Dad, Poor Dad*, you'll become familiar with this once you start doing it, but the smartest way to get rich slowly is through investment properties. The tax code is written in an appealing way to owning investment property that it is almost unfair. It's crazy how different it is for someone who gets investment income through property rather than investment income through other sources. Since the tax consequences are just so terrible with other investment strategies, while when you own property the depreciation really wipes most of the income until you sell it.

Now there is a point where depreciation runs out which is 27.5 years now, and at that point then you start making decisions on, is this something you still want to continue to hold and potentially pay a little bit of income tax? Or do you want to sell it and take the gain in which case it does become taxable.

Susan: Can you make it your primary residence to offset that?

Tyler: Yes, there are some tricks to reduce your tax consequences. You can do what's called a 1031 exchange. You take the equity that occurred from the sale of the home and then you have to identify a new home within a few months of closing on the duplex or whatever you're selling to move that equity into. As long as that equity is moved into the next property then the 1031 exchange works, if for some reason it does not, then it becomes a taxable event.

Why It's More Expensive to Rent than to Own a Home...

Susan: Is owning a home more expensive than renting?

Tyler: That's a great question because with owning a home comes more responsibility; now you're not living in someone else's house, you're living in your house.

The way I look at it is, let's say you've got a rental car. If you got something that's broken on a rental car, you take it back to the rental place, and you'd say "Hey your car broke; you better fix it!" and you can walk away from it. Whereas if you own the home, there's no "place" to take your house back to. You *are* the company in that situation. If something breaks on your home, you are responsible for it.

From the perspective of maintenance and responsibility, owning a home is something that you really need to be in a situation where you are comfortable taking on those responsibilities. From my experience with most people who are seeking the options of home ownership, they are at that point in their life where they're responsible adults. They're ready to take that next step and responsibility, and if something needs to be repaired they're okay with writing a small check to make that repair.

The beauty of owning a home with *The Rent-Free Solution* is you're going to have such a small payment or no payment to begin with. If you do a good job with your house inspection, you shouldn't have a lemon of a house. And when expenses do come up, you're going to be in a situation where you're financially capable of handling those expenses while most people may not be.

Susan: In other words if you did the traditional route of just owning a home and living in it by yourself, there could be more expenses, but with your way the cash flow offsets it. Since you're having so much extra cash here, either from cheaper rent or earning income from renters, you can set aside some of that money toward monthly maintenance and repairs that are going to come up down the road.

Tyler: Yes it definitely could, and then to expand on that question "Is owning a home more expensive than renting?" A lot of people have the impression overall that the monthly payment would be more expensive. Even if you don't utilize *The Rent-Free Solution* and you just do a regular house, and you buy it rather than renting, in a lot of cases you still can own a home for less than what you spend on a monthly basis renting right now. Even if after reading through all of these examples you still don't think that it is something you want to do, owning a home is still in a lot of cases less expensive than renting.

By taking *The Rent Free Solution*, you can see that living in a place for $100 or earning an additional $300 a month income is definitely cheaper than renting. It's very hard to make an argument otherwise. There are multiple levels of implementation on this, but I would say no matter what, you will be in a better situation than you would have by owning rather than renting.

Susan: This isn't like you have to suffer through this for seven years and then it will start paying off; you'll save money in the first month.

Tyler: Not at all. It's a great option to just implement this quickly because it's not like there's some crazy long breakeven point where it begins to make sense. I mean you can really begin to make sense of this from the day you move in.

What to Do If You Have Credit Issues...

Susan: What about someone that doesn't have the best credit score, do you have to have a better credit score to qualify for this?

Tyler: That's a great question. When you go to buy a house, credit is a part of the equation, and part of determining if you can qualify to buy the house or not.

The quick and dirty answer to that is credit scores can range anywhere from 300 to 850, 850 being best and 300 being worst, and if you have a credit score of 620 or better you'll likely qualify for a loan based on your credit.

Now if you have something that's less than 620, the good news is that it's not difficult to improve your credit score. You just need the advice of an expert to tell you what needs to be done. This book isn't about credit repair; I don't want to go too deep into that. I will say this, if we work with the client and they don't qualify the day that they talk with us, we'll help them put together a game plan to get them to a situation where they'll qualify.

Credit score wise, 620 is a minimum point. The one thing I have to mention is that getting your credit score isn't as easy as going to one of those websites you hear about on television.

It's really good to have a mortgage professional pull your credit score, because they'll pull a mortgage specific credit report, which is different than if you're going to get an auto loan or something else. Once you know where your credit stands, you know if your credit score is where it needs to be, but I will tell you this 620 is not an excellent credit score; the average nationally is about 720.

Susan: What about someone that maybe has a foreclosure or a bankruptcy on their credit report? What are their options?

Tyler: Foreclosure and bankruptcy happen for a lot of different reasons. The first thing for us is determining if it was due to extenuating circumstances, things like loss of a job or medical bills or death of someone in the family. There are circumstances where you can make exceptions to the rules on the timing for this kind of thing. I will say that if you had a bankruptcy, there are lenders that allow you to get a loan if you are two years out of bankruptcy. A lot of people think its seven years. So, two years is usually the time frame on bankruptcy.

Then if you're talking about foreclosure, which means you're a homeowner at one point for whatever reason you lost the home to the bank. That time frame is usually three years from the date the foreclosure actually happened. Again a lot of people think that it's seven or more years for foreclosure.

On bankruptcy, if it's two years out we're fine. If it's less than two years, and there are circumstances we can explain, then you might be able to do it sooner than that. With a foreclosure, that's three years out from the day the foreclosure and again we can do less if there's a circumstance that we can explain that caused it.

Susan: Very good, and I have to say from talking to some international people that as a rule in America anyway, we're a pretty forgiving country as far as credit goes.

In some places on the planet, if you have a foreclosure or a bankruptcy that's it. You're done. You'll never get another home. It's like a one shot thing. Here seems like, okay pay your penance for a few years, and then you're right back in the game.

Tyler: Yes, it's a very forgiving place, and the cool thing is people who've been through that kind of thing, they know what it took to get there. They don't want to go back. They deserve a second chance.

I've had many, many clients who've been through some extremely difficult situations, and after talking to them they've been some of the best borrowers, so to speak, lowest risk borrowers that there were. Underwriters understand that, mortgage companies understand that and I understand that. So it's really fun to help someone go from a place where they were at a really, really low point in their life. We can help them get to a point where they do qualify if they don't qualify at the moment they came to us.

How Much Down Payment Do I Need?

Susan: Earlier you mentioned one of the concerns people have is coming up with a large down payment. How large of a down payment do people need?

Tyler: That's a great question, and it's very much dependent on the type of loan you get, and I don't want to go through all the different loans scenarios and overwhelm anyone at this stage.

I will tell you that there are programs out there that require no down payments, like literally zero money down. But, it's not a broad based thing, so not everybody will qualify, and not every property will qualify. These zero down loans are the worst-case type situation. I like to tell people, as a first time buyer, you have to have three and half percent down. On a $100,000 you're talking about $3500.

The really cool part about that money is that it can come from a lot of different places. If you have it in a checking or savings account, that's fantastic, but if you don't have it easily accessible, you can also access things like a 401(k). You can get maybe a 401(k) loan or withdraw that money.

Another popular option is a gift since a lot of people want to see them become homeowners. It's something that's really exciting especially for parents to see their kid buy their first house. It's not uncommon for mom and dad to want to help provide that down payment or a part of that down payment. That small three and a half percent down payment can come from a family member or someone close to that person. Gifted down payments are quite common, so the down payment could range anywhere from literally nothing down if you find the right property, to as little and three and a half percent down which is more appealing.

Susan: What about someone just out of college, do they have to wait a certain number of years before they take advantage of this?

Tyler: Excellent question, and I think a lot of people think that they have to wait until they've been at a job for two years to be able to buy a house.

The truth is college counts as work history for the loan programs that we offer. If you've been in school as a student and maybe you haven't worked at all the whole time you've been a student or maybe you've worked but haven't been in the same line of work that you're current occupation is, it doesn't matter.

The beauty of getting a loan now as a first time home buyer with *The Rent-Free Solution* loans we offer, is that you can buy a home and literally have just started that job or even better, only have an offer letter, you're graduating next week, and you start the following week. You can buy a home just based on a formal offer of a job.

We're experts with first time home buyers, and some companies may not be familiar with this, but I'm here to tell you that even if you just started the job or not even started the job but just got an offer for a job straight out of college, you can absolutely qualify for a home.

How to Safeguard Yourself from Major Repairs...

Susan: What if someone is not mechanically inclined and they are concerned about all the things that can break in a home. What do you recommend to them?

Tyler: I am an expert in this area because I'm about the least handy person you'll ever meet. As a homeowner, I've always relied on friends who've been able to fix mechanical issues. It's always surprising if you put it up on Facebook. "Hey my sink is leaking, does anybody know a good plumber or is anybody a plumber?" "Oh, I will come over and help for a beer; I'll help you fix it." Or somebody is actually naming specific plumbing companies that can help fix things. I think people underestimate the value of crowd sourcing answers and support for people. That having been said, if you're not wanting to rely on other people, there are many people who are completely capable of fixing things for a reasonable fee.

I will tell you that renting a home or renting an apartment some call a maintenance person. Assuming that place doesn't stink at what they do, that maintenance person will get there on short notice, and you don't have to pay anything for it, but based on my experience in working with investment property owners, you are paying for it.

Part of our qualifying them to do a loan is estimating that they're going to have maintenance expenses. I can tell you right now that they do budget for it, and it is built into your rent, so if you want to look at it that way you might as well add $50 a month to have a rainy day fund when something breaks.

I think a lot of people over-think that there are usually a lot more people that you know that could help you than you realized; you just kind of crowd source it. My personal opinion is just post it on Facebook. I've been able to solve a lot of problems through Facebook.

Susan: If you buy the right house like you mentioned that earlier you should do your homework. If you buy a home that has had the maintenance done on it, there's a better chance things aren't going to be breaking willy-nilly.

Tyler: To be clear, there's a way you can safe guard yourself from major repairs. At the time that you buy a home, you can buy a warranty, which is an insurance policy against the worst happening. You can even ask for the home sellers to pay for this. It's pretty common requesting the seller to pay for the cost of a home warranty. It goes year to year, but if something major happens like a furnace goes down or the dishwasher craps out or the refrigerator stops working for example, the warranty will cover it.

Home warranties are made specifically to apply a solution and pay for that solution by paying a small deductible. That's another backup option. If you're a homeowner, you can buy a home warranty and just renew it every year if you're fearful of any major expenses or really do know that something major is going to happen in a short term. For some people getting a home warranty is the best option.

Susan: Because of the way you're recommending they buy the house using *The Rent-Free Solution*, they're going to have the cash flow, so if you're thinking about it now, like I won't have the money for repairs, well you potentially have as much as whatever you're paying in rent now it just put towards it. You'll actually have more cash hanging around for maintenance and repairs

Tyler: Absolutely.

Susan: How does someone go about finding a good mortgage company because it's kind of a scary world for us? People don't buy homes very often, so this isn't an area that we're actually very familiar with.

Tyler: The key is finding a good person to work with because just like anything there's good and bad. My ultimate recommendation for finding a good mortgage professional is to work by referrals. If someone has highly recommended someone, they are a good person to start with. If you're more of a do it yourselfer, which I know I am, I usually go online and just research people. If you were to go online and search Des Moines mortgage lenders, Google has a lot of online reviews.

I will say just as a personal selfish plug that if you go and look at Des Moines area mortgage lenders online, we've had over 140 people who've worked with us leave positive reviews. Online reviewers provide their experiences very transparently. It's really helped to build a lot of confidence for people on why they open up a conversation with us.

If you do research on any company online, you'll quickly realize if they do any business, they'll have reviews and what those customers have to say about their experience. That's the first thing that I recommend doing. The second thing is finding what questions to ask mortgage people while you're talking with them.

Now the first thing is you're going to want to work with somebody who's familiar with executing the homeowner strategy you want to do. If you say, "Hey are you familiar with *The Rent-Free Solution*?" and they say no, you might want to run the other direction because if they don't understand how to execute what we're talking about it's going to be really difficult to get through the process without a little bit of help. It's really important you're working with someone who has that experience around that particular topic.

The next thing you have to understand is the different types of mortgage people that are out there. Because in Des Moines, just here in Central Iowa, there's probably over 2000 loan officers that can help you get a mortgage, but out of those 2000 you can put those 2000 people into one of three different buckets if you really want to simplify it.

The first group of people that you can work with includes banks and credit unions, and the way you know you're working with a banker or a credit union is when you walk in the door you see that they have a teller line. They take your deposits and put money into your checking and savings accounts. The big advantage of working with a banker or credit union is they ultimately do all of their underwriting and everything in their own offices, so the loan isn't being outsourced to other people; they take care of everything under one roof which is nice.

The second thing that's really nice about banks and credit unions is they do portfolio type loans which may not help you at all, depending on who you are as a reader. What I will say is if you're a person who doesn't qualify for a regular mortgage which you'd find out if you started talking with a mortgage professional, banks and credit unions can sometimes do loans for people that wouldn't normally be able to get loans, so that's good to know. The downsides of working with the bank or credit unions is they only have one outlet for loans, so you're not going to go to a large bank and have that large bank sell you a loan to another large bank. They don't want to have that competition with the other bank for your checking and savings accounts, so when you walk into a local bank they're going to get you a loan with that local bank. If that local bank gets very competitive on that day, the interest rates that you will receive probably won't be very competitive either.

The second bucket of people that you would talk with is mortgage brokers, and to be honest mortgage brokers, for the most part, are pretty hard to find anymore, because it's just a very difficult environment to work in. I used to be a mortgage broker, so I'm extremely familiar with it. The advantage of working with a mortgage broker is they tend to have a lot of different outlets for getting you a loan. It's not uncommon for mortgage broker to work with up to 200 different banks. Anytime they quote an interest rate, they shop at all 200 of those banks but they tend to be very competitive. The downsides of being a mortgage broker or working with a mortgage broker is that you have them outsourcing everything. They don't do anything in house; their role is really to play kind of middleman between you and the company that you're getting a loan from, so sometimes you'll get a loan that's for Des Moines, Iowa that's been underwritten in San Diego, California.

I don't know about you, but I think there's pretty big difference between Des Moines, Iowa and San Diego, California, and once you go to get a loan from someone in San Diego, California you realize that they just don't really understand how things work here in Des Moines. When you're working with a mortgage broker, it tends to be kind of a fragmented experience in the getting of the loan because you have people who aren't familiar with the area underwriting the law, so that's kind of the big downside of working with a mortgage broker.

Now the third bucket of people that you would work with is correspondent banks. Correspondent banks are people who are kind of a hybrid of banks and credit unions and mortgage brokers. Correspondent banks work with several banks. I'm a correspondent banker, so we work with 21 different banks. In any given program, any given loan we're working with the client on, we can shop 21 different banks to make sure we're getting the clients the best deal.

The other thing is you also have all the underwriting still in house. With the correspondent bank they do all their underwriting, so they're familiar with the people that are working with the loan. You don't get blindsided by random requests from the underwriter.

The downside, to be fair, of working with a correspondent banker is they don't have any in-house products. If you're a person who doesn't fit in the box, so to speak, a correspondent banker probably won't be the person to get you the best loan. What will commonly happen is if you start to search for somebody like a correspondent banker, and they aren't the best fit for you, usually they'll connect you with a person who would be a better solution if it is out there.

Those are the three different types of people that you can get a loan from, and again there are thousands of people that fit into each one of those three categories. It is just good to have a good understanding of what those choices are, and what the pros and cons of each of them are.

Susan: Is there a cost of waiting to buying now versus if they decide to wait and until 2020 to buy a house?

Tyler: It's a common question. People are always fearful of making a decision quickly, and some people should wait. I want to be clear. Not everybody should buy a house immediately. Once you have a conversation with the loan officer, you'll determine if it is really the right time.

It's also important to know the impact of rising interest rates on your affordability. For example if you qualified for a $200,000 home today, the current rate as I write this book is 4%. Let' say you buy today at 4%, and you qualify for $200,000, if the rates go up to 5%, which everybody that knows anything about the economy is in agreement that the interest rates will rise. They certainly are not going to stay at four percent forever. When interest rates rise the 5% could happen in just a few months really when they start rising. That affordability will be hugely impacted; your preapproval would go from a $200,000 home down to $180,000 home just with that one percent increase in rates. That's 10%!

Here's the rule of thumb, if you want to have a little take away that you can remember, for every 1% increase in interest rates, it's an impact of 10% in your home affordability. That surprises a lot of people because it's a pretty drastic change, but it really does impact things. Just remember, even though you might qualify/afford much more, your payment will move drastically as rates rise.

Susan: You're saying if interest rates go from 4% to 5%, my affordability, if I could afford $150,000 home prior to that now I may only qualify for a $135,000 home?

Tyler: Correct and going on with the same point of view, if you have a home that you want to buy, let's say you qualify for a whole lot more than $200,000, but you want to buy that $200,000 home. That $200,000 home becomes 10% more expensive to you when interest rates rise that 1% too, so it doesn't just affect your affordability, it also affects your actual monthly cost.

In this situation since we've talked so much about how the long term impact of interest rates changing and becoming more expensive will drastically change your cash flow. Over time, it will impact your lifetime value of that investment. If you're in a situation where you can qualify, and now is the right time for you to buy, it would pain me to watch you sit on the sideline and wait and watch interest rates increase. It could really cost you a lot of money.

How Much House Can I Afford?

Susan: How can I find out how much house I can afford, especially when you try and factor in the cost of an additional income source? How can someone figure that out?

Tyler: There are a lot of complexities to knowing what you qualify for, and to be completely honest with you, there's a lot of websites that put themselves out there as a great resource to figure out home affordability. I'll tell you from personal experience that a lot of these websites are really not reliable.

The best way to figure out what you can afford is to talk with a mortgage professional to figure out what type of loan you'll be doing, how much money you're comfortable putting down, then working that backwards to determine what's going to fit in your budget, what they will actually give you a loan for versus what you actually want to spend.

I think the thing that most people are surprised by once they start the conversation with us as their mortgage professional is that, they determine they qualify for a whole lot more than what they want to spend which is great news. It's fun to know that you qualified for a mortgage, and at the same time it's good to know what your limits are personally too. Just because you can buy a $200,000 home doesn't necessarily mean you want to actually do it. You might find yourself eating Ramen Noodles and hot dogs for the rest of your life.

Susan: Good point.

Tyler: *The Rent-Free Solution* has been able to help people understand how rental income impacts the affordability. Unfortunately, many mortgage professionals don't realize how you can utilize the rental income to help offset you monthly expense. They may goof up telling you how much you can afford. They might tell you that you actually afford less. So it's a selfish statement but working with someone who's familiar with *The Rent-Free Solution* becomes extremely important when it comes to the details as how the implementation works. What you can afford becomes a big piece of that implementation.

The Difference between Being Pre-Qualified and Pre-Approved for a Home?

Susan: What is the difference between pre-qualified and being pre-approved?

Tyler: They are two very similar sounding words aren't they?

Susan: Yes.

Tyler: It's drastic what the difference and the meaning is. To be prequalified means that someone's had a verbal conversation with you or you've given certain inputs of information. They've said "Oh yeah generally speaking it should be fine", but the danger of saying generally speaking you should be fine is that there are so many different small things that could totally sideline being qualified to buy a home. I want to make sure that any reader knows where you're not going after a prequalification.

Before you buy a house you want to be preapproved. Before you even start looking at houses you want to be preapproved because a preapproval will tell you specifically what you qualify for; it will tell you if you need any more documentation to make sure that there aren't any hiccups in the process of buying a house, also to make sure that there aren't any surprises in the process of buying a house. A lot of people who you hear having negative experiences of buying a home, usually if you really got down to the bottom layer of the issues, they were prequalified, not truly preapproved when they went to make that decision to buy a home.

Unfortunately a lot of mortgage companies don't take any time to distinguish the difference between the two, and the truth is because we don't get paid to issue preapprovals or prequalification. A lot of companies don't put much focus on that, but for me I think your experience buying a home is priority one to me. I want to make sure you have an extremely good experience. Being preapproved is how you deliver that experience. Being prequalified sets you up for nothing but disappointments.

Susan: The home sellers would want to look for the preapproval buyer over the prequalified.

Tyler: They definitely want to be seen as a preapproved buyer.

Susan: If you're especially competing with other buyers it may set you apart.

Tyler: Yes absolutely it will.

What Goes into a Mortgage Payment?

Susan: What makes up a mortgage payment?

Tyler: When you buy a house there's a few things you're paying for as part of your monthly payment. There's the loan itself, which is the principle and interest portion of the payment. That's just going to pay what you borrowed to purchase the home.

The next portion is property taxes. Being a property owner here in Central Iowa, you'll pay property taxes to the county that home resides in. You pay a certain amount of money each month that goes to Polk County for example, and that will be part of your mortgage payment.

The third part of your mortgage payment is homeowners insurance, and homeowners insurance pays to replace contents or rebuild the home if they were to have any major damage through fire, natural disaster or theft; that kind of thing.

If you buy a home with a lower down payment, you could potentially pay private mortgage insurance, and that's commonly known as PMI. PMI is something that you pay as part of your mortgage payment. This protects the lender in the event that you default on the loan.

If you buy a condo or a townhouse you could also potentially pay association dues as part of your payment, and when you hear people talk about mortgage payments, a lot of times you'll hear the term or acronym PITI.

If you've heard of PITI it stands for Principle, Interest, Taxes and Insurance, so if you hear somebody say "Oh is that a PITI payment?", the goal with PITI is that's all inclusive. Usually PITI also includes any mortgage insurance that you're paying, although it's not part of the acronym, and it should include association, but again it's not part of the acronym.

The mortgage payment itself goes to pay those things, and then outside of the mortgage much like renting you'll continue to pay things like your utility bills, or heating, air-conditioning, electrical, and a water bill. If you pay a garbage bill, maybe that's part of you water bill. Those things will be extra: cable television, telephone that kind of thing.

Here's How the Rent-Free Solution Works...

Susan: Is there a way for someone to find out what a rent free home looks like?

Tyler: So we've created a list actually if you're in central Iowa, not just Des Moines, but bordering suburbs of Des Moines. And, we can come up with a rent-free list in whatever area you're looking at as long as it is here in Central Iowa. If you're looking outside of Iowa, we can refer you to a loan officer who is familiar with *The Rent-Free Solution* in your area. To make a rent-free home, the key is for you to make sure you buy a home that has the potential to pull in enough rent.

To offset the mortgage, you also want to find a home that has enough space to able to make it a rent-free home. You don't want to buy a small place that doesn't have the ability to add renters easily. We have come up with a list of what we think makes the best rent free homes.

The best way to get in contact with me to get a copy of that free list is to just send me an email to tyler@tylerosbyteam.com and then just in the subject line put Rent-Free Home List. I can send you a PDF of everything that's currently available. So you can take a look and see what's out there right now.

Susan: Very good because I think that actually will be very eye opening for people to see that we're not talking about buying a dump in a bad area of town and suffering for the next 10 years.

Tyler: Yeah there are a lot of extremely nice properties that would fit in with this criteria, and we can definitely help you find one.

Susan: If someone has questions how can they get in touch with you?

Tyler: If you just have a question, you could email me. That's the fastest response time. The email address is tyler@tylerosbyteam.com. You can also call my office if you like which is 515-257-6729, and my extension is "5".

If you're really thinking that *The Rent-Free Solution* might be something you're interested in, and you want to just go over a bit deeper on what this would mean to me, you can help me crunch the numbers that sort of thing. We can definitely do that for you.

We have a unique offer that we do for people who are trying to get those feet wet, maybe they're not really sure if now is the time or not. It's our Free Home Loan Report, and the free home loan report is different than anything else you've probably seen from a mortgage company. We're not going to try to get you preapproved at this point; we're not going to try to get you to jump through a bunch of hoops like most mortgage companies do. We're just going to help you figure out the answers to the questions you probably have. Like how much can I afford? How much down payment do I need? What do need to know about this process? What would my payments be?

We can prepare that for you with the Free Home Loan Report, and again there's no charge to that. The website that you go to is **www.iowahomeloanreport.com.**

From there, all the instructions are at the website to get us the form of information that we need to continue that conversation. It takes roughly 10 minutes to get us the information we'll need to prepare your customized Free Home Loan Report.

The second thing is we have that list of Rent-Free homes. These are extremely nice to have access to. You'll know exactly what's on the market here in Central Iowa which fit the criteria that we outlined here in this book. Again just send me an email to Tyler@TylerOsbyTeam.com with "Rent-Free Home List".

Then the third thing is we can help partner you with an experienced REALTOR here in Central Iowa who's familiar with The Rent-Free Solution. We'll be able to help you find the right house to achieve your goal of owning a home, but more importantly owning a Rent-Free Home, and we can help you connect with that person.

Susan: Yes, I want thank you. This is super exciting because I think, it's like you said earlier, it's not something that is being taught. Certainly not free of charge anyway, you may have to pay for a seminar and learn these strategies. I think its super exciting. There may be a way to both buy a home and start saving money every month, but at the same time you can take care of your future, at least a big chunk of your future. I think that's super exciting. Thank you so much for sharing this with us Tyler.

Tyler: Yes, I appreciate the opportunity to share the concept, and I'm just looking forward to seeing more success stories, which is really fun to see people become home owners in situations where they didn't see themselves doing it before and really setting up a long term plan.

Here's How to Stop Renting and Buy a Home in Des Moines and Live Rent-Free...

You already know owning a home is big part of the American Dream. The confusing part is not knowing how to find one that doesn't cost more than renting (or even better, almost living free, rent-free).

That's where we come in. We help people just like you find and purchase their homes and live Rent-Free.

Option One: Get a list of rent free homes that are currently available by going to www.rentfreehomefinder.com ($50 value).

Option Two: Get your free home loan report by going to www.iowahomeloanreport.com ($300 value).

Option Three: Attend our Ultimate Home Buying Workshop for first time homebuyers at no cost ($20 value). Learn more at www.ultimatehomebuyingworkshop.com/rentfree

Most people think it takes flawless credit, a large down payment and a larger monthly expense to buy a home.

With *The Rent-Free Solution*, you'll learn why these often are not true.

If you'd like us to help, just send an email to: tyler@tylerosbyteam.com.

About the Author

Tyler Osby is the father of daughter Piper, born in November 2013. He's also the husband of a beautiful young lady named Heather, and the son of two great parents who raised him in Central Iowa. He loves fast cars and is the pickiest eater you'll ever meet!
He has over 25,000 songs on his iPod. He also has a Vizsla (a very energetic dog breed) named George that will likely have a children's book written about him some day called "George's Bad Decisions."

In business, Tyler is the branch manager and a certified mortgage planner with the Tyler Osby Team at Fairway Independent Mortgage. They are a local mortgage company that has a huge focus on education and working with first time home buyers. His team is best known for quick and informative loan approvals while forming long lasting friendships with their clients. They may close loans fast, but they won't treat you like a number. On time. Under budget. With no surprises.

www.ingramcontent.com/pod-product-compliance
Lightning Source LLC
Chambersburg PA
CBHW071810170526
45167CB00003B/1248